Yvan's Workshop

Smoothies and Co.

Cooking with a Juicer

Yvan's Workshop

Smoothies and Co.

Cooking with a Juicer

/ Recipes: Yvan Cadiou /
/ Photographs: Jean-Pierre and Valentin Duval /
/ Recipe editing and lay-out: Marie-Alexandre Perraud /
/ Translation: Anne Trager /

Romain Pages Publishing

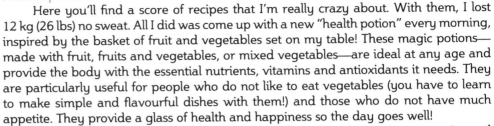

Health potions

Here you'll find a score of recipes that I'm really crazy about. With them, I lost 12 kg (26 lbs) no sweat. All I did was come up with a new "health potion" every morning, inspired by the basket of fruit and vegetables set on my table! These magic potions—made with fruit, fruits and vegetables, or mixed vegetables—are ideal at any age and provide the body with the essential nutrients, vitamins and antioxidants it needs. They are particularly useful for people who do not like to eat vegetables (you have to learn to make simple and flavourful dishes with them!) and those who do not have much appetite. They provide a glass of health and happiness so the day goes well!

In our society, work is so much less physical than it was in previous centuries and it is essential that we pay attention to our bodies, that we be careful not to eat too much and that we exercise. The obesity that today plagues adults and children is largely due to overuse of "added sugar" and constant snacking. Yet, both can be avoided. Drinking fruit and vegetable juice in the morning or at meals acts like "medication" that is not only healthy and useful for the body, giving it vitality, but also happens to do away with the desire to keep snacking.

Breakfast is the most important meal of the day, both for intellectual endeavours and physical development. My 13-year-old daughter Alta is a perfect illustration of why I needed to win this "battle" for balanced a balanced diet that includes fruit and vegetables. If I were to leave her to her own devices, she would go to school every day with only a bird-sized meal, even though a child of her age is constantly growing, has a long day of studies in front of her and needs energy for her body starting when she gets up in the morning. This is what motivates me to create on a daily basis: finding the ideal equations that allow me to nourish her and amuse her with a large glass of juice.

It is often recommended that we consume five to ten portions of fruits and vegetables a day. A glass with 25 to 40 cl (9 to 16 fl oz/1 to 2 cups) of fresh juice provides about two thirds of the vitamins and nutrients we need for the day. Of course, you should not neglect to include whole, cooked fruits and vegetables in your diet, because juice has less fibre and minerals. Adding honey (a natural sweetener that the body can assimilate directly), royal jelly, pollen or even natural grains in your juices bestows on them even more virtues to build a healthy body. I used to be pretty much a hypochondriac, but today, thanks to my morning "potions" and of course more generally the way I eat, I'm full of beans! Or cool as a cucumber, depending… So, cheers!

Some recommendations

Use fruits and vegetables that are in season.

Prefer produce that has little or no treatment. If you do, you will not have to peel it, and washing will be enough. Peel citrus fruit and a few others: pineapples, thick-skinned avocados, melons, and the like. You can also add a little citrus skin in the centrifuge juicer to add a tang.

Do not drink too much citrus in the morning: the acidity is hard on an empty stomach.

If possible, juice the fruits and vegetables right before you drink them: air and light are quick to destroy the vitamins. If you keep the juice a few hours, protect it in a sealed bottle. You can add a little lemon juice on the top to avoid oxidation.

You can thicken juices with a little ground almond or some banana, either puréed or crushed with a fork.

Feel free to explore fruit and vegetable compositions, so that you can choose those you body needs most at various moments in your life.

Tricks of the trade…

Modern centrifuge juicers accept large pieces of fruit and vegetables, so you do not need to cut them up into pieces any smaller than what you need to get through the tube that feeds the machine. Some ingredients, such as avocados, bananas, beets, papayas, mangos, have to go through the machine alternately with harder, juicier ingredients, whose juice will "rinse through" their thick pulp.

Once you have made the juice, mix it well until it is smooth, and blend it to make it foamy. Some juices can separate after a few minutes (because the various ingredients have different densities). You can use a wooden spoon to mix the juice without touching the foam: delicately dip it in the glass and then turn the handle between the palms of your hands.

If you want impeccable glasses, clean them with steam: hold them aver the spout of a kettle, and then wipe dry with a clean kitchen towel.

…and some comments about the book

The recipes are listed in the following order: mainly vegetable juices, fruit and vegetable combos, mainly fruit juices, and then cocktails.

Most of the juices are very quick to prepare and so no preparation time is indicated. Time indications are given for recipes prepared with the juices.

I chose to use low cooking temperatures in the juice-based recipes in order to respect as much as possible the nutritional elements found in the fruits and vegetables.

Recipes

approx.
50 cl
18 fl oz
2 cups

/ Going for a Dip /

Ingredients

- 7 young carrots + 2 to dip
- 2 blood oranges
- ½ vanilla pod
- 1 small dice fresh curcuma
  or 1 small pinch ground curcuma
- a few drops of argan oil

Peel the oranges. Wash the carrots. Juice them with the fresh curcuma if you have it. Split the vanilla pod lengthwise and scrape out the grains with a knife. Add to the juice along with a few drops of argan oil and the ground curcuma if that is what you are using. Whisk. Serve the glasses with a carrot for dipping.

 x 4 to 6

/ Carrot Cube Hors-d'oeuvres /

Preparation: 10 minutes
Set aside: around 30 minutes

Ingredients

- 50 cl/18 fl oz/2 cups
  Going for a Dip juice
- 1 teaspoon agar agar powder
- 1 small branch celery
- a few sprigs of parsley
- salt and pepper

Heat half of the Going for a Dip juice until simmering—do not allow it to boil (heat to around 80°C/175°F). Season lightly with salt and pepper. Add a few sprigs of parsley and a small, chopped celery stick. Add the agar agar powder and whisk. Remove from heat, add the remaining juice and mix. Pour into a dish large enough to make cubes your chosen thickness. Once the jelly has cooled down, cut into cubes and serve.

/ Agar agar is derived from seaweed and has powerful jellying properties (is about seven times stronger than animal gelatine). It comes in powdered form. It melts when placed in a liquid that is 80°C/175°F, and then gels at 25°C/77°F. It makes entirely natural jellies. They have a very firm, pleasant texture, and can lend themselves to imaginative variations, such as jellied cocktails served in strips. Try this with a piña colada (see page 86) or a Bloody Mary (tomato juice and vodka). /

approx.
60 cl
1 ¼ pints
2 ½ cups

/ Fennel Tonic /

Ingredients

- 1 bulb fennel
- 2 or 3 tomatoes
- 1 sweet apple (Golden)
- ½ celery rib
- 2 cardamom pods
- salt and pepper

Wash the vegetables and fruit, process them through the juicer, and then season lightly with salt and pepper. Open the cardamom pods and recuperate the small seeds they contain. Crush them with a pestle. Chop the fennel leaves, mix with the cardamom and use to decorate the glasses of juice.

11

approx.
70 cl
1⅓ pints
3 cups

/ Really Instant Soup /

Ingredients

- 2 bunches fresh watercress
- 2 sweet apples (Golden)
- 1 handful fresh bean sprouts (mung)
- 1 bulb fennel
- 1 small piece fresh ginger
- salt and pepper

Remove the large watercress stems. Wash all the ingredients and juice them. Season with salt and pepper and serve.

/ Mung bean sprouts are commonly referred to as ibean sproutsî. Mung beans (*Vigna Radiata*) are different from soya beans (*Glycine Max*), which are used to make tofu, soy drinks and the like. Sometimes mung beans are referred to as green soy, by they do not have the proteins or reputation of soya beans. Their nutritional value is closer to that of a green vegetable. You can make them yourself by sprouting mung beans. /

x 4 to 6

Preparation: 10 minutes
Freeze: at least 2 hours

Ingredients

- 70 cl/ 1⅓ pints Really Instant Soup juice
- a few tablespoons of white sugar
- a few tablespoons of mint syrup

Pour the Really Instant Soup juice in a flat, stainless steel recipient and put it in the freezer for 2 to 3 hours. Once the preparation freezes, use a fork to scrape of flakes. Serve or store in the freezer. To serve, place a little sugar in a small plate and mint syrup in another. Dip the rim of the glasses in the syrup, and then in the sugar to decorate them. Fill the glasses with the granita and serve.

approx.
70 cl
1⅓ pints
3 cups

/ Rocket Juice /

Ingredients

- 4 tomatoes
- 2 celery ribs
- 2 large handfuls rocket
- juice of ½ lemon
- 1 dash olive oil
- salt and pepper

Wash the vegetables and run them through the juicer. Season with lemon juice, olive oil, salt and pepper. Serve.

/ The strong flavour of the rocket dominates this Italian-style juice. Serve it as you would a gazpacho: for a meal, with a salad or a sandwich. /

x 4 to 6

/ Rocket and Comté Risotto /

Preparation: 10 minutes
Cooking time: around 25 minutes

Ingredients

- 70 cl/1⅓ pints/3 cups Rocket Juice
- 300 g/10½ oz/1⅓ cup arborio rice or other risotto rice
- 125 g/4⅓ oz comté cheese
- 2 or 3 tomatoes
- 1 sweet onion
- 1 clove garlic
- 1 sprig fresh thyme
- a few sprigs fresh basil
- 15 cl/5 fl oz/⅗ cup vegetable or chicken stock, or diluted soup
- 1 dash olive oil
- salt and pepper

Peel the onion and garlic and chop finely. Cook them in the olive oil until soft but not brown. Add the rice and a sprig of thyme. Mix and add the stock. Allow the rice to absorb the liquid, and then add the Rocket Juice little by little, allowing the rice to absorb it each time. Cut the tomatoes into a dice. Chop the basil leaves. Grate the cheese. Just before the rice is finished cooking, add the grated cheese so it can melt. The risotto should be creamy. If needed, add juice, stock or water. Season with salt and pepper. Before serving, add the tomato dice and the chopped basil. Sprinkle with a dash of olive oil.

approx.
80 cl
1 ½ pints
3 ½ cups

/ Spanish Sun /

Ingredients

- 4 tomatoes
- ½ cucumber
- ½ red bell pepper
- 1 sweet onion
- 2 cloves garlic
- 1 piece slightly stale bread
- olive oil
- salt and pepper

Wash the tomatoes, cucumber and bell pepper. Remove the pepper seeds. Peel the onion and garlic. Put all these ingredients through the juicer. Cut the bread into a dice. Sprinkle with olive oil and season with salt and pepper. Serve the juice in glasses, adding the bread dice. Decorate with an herb sprig.

/ This is the very essence of gazpacho, with no frills, served with flavoured croutons. /

x 4 to 6

/ Gazpacho Granita with Baked Apple /

Preparation: 20 minutes
Cooking time: 15 to 20 minutes
Freeze: at least 2 hours

Ingredients

- 80 cl/1½ pints/3½ cups Spanish Sun
- 1 small, flavourful apple per person
- 50 g/1¾ oz/3 tablespoons butter

Set aside a little Spanish Sun to decorate the plates. Pour the rest in a flat, stainless steel recipient and put it in the freezer for 2 to 3 hours. Once the preparation freezes, use a fork to scrape off flakes. Serve or store in the freezer. Preheat the oven to 180°C/350°F/gas 5. Use a knife to make a shallow incision around the apples so they do not burst when baked. Place them in a baking dish with a large dollop of butter and bake for 15 to 20 minutes. Cool; open with a knife. Hollow the apples out a little and top with a scoop of granita. Cover with the apple top.

approx.
60 cl
1 ¼ pints
2 ½ cups

/ Vitamin Fix /

Ingredients

- 1 courgette (zucchini)
- ½ cucumber
- ½ green bell pepper
- 1 celery rib
- ½ Granny Smith apple
- 1 sweet apple (Golden)
- ½ lime
- salt and pepper

Wash all the ingredients. Remove the seeds from the green pepper. Peel the lime, removing the pith and the outside membranes. Process everything in the juicer. Season lightly with salt and pepper. Serve with a rib of celery.

x 4 to 6

/ Vitamin Fix Mussel and Clam Stew /

Preparation: 15 minutes
Cooking time: around 5 minutes

Ingredients

- 60 cl/1¼ pints/2½ cups
  Vitamin Fix juice
- 1½ kg /3 lb 6 oz mussels
- 500 g/1 lb 2 oz clams or cockles
- 1 small bunch parsley
- pepper

Clean the mussels and clams. Pour into a large pot with a glass of water. Heat until they begin to open. Immediately add the Vitamin Fix juice and continue to cook over low heat for 2 to 3 minutes. Add pepper and chopped parsley. Serve.

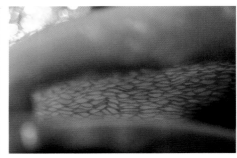

approx.
50 cl
18 fl oz
2 cups

/ Red Salad Smoothie /

Ingredients

- 1 thick-leafed lettuce, such as romaine
- 3 or 4 young carrots
- 2 cooked beetroots
- 1 lemon
- salt and pepper

Peel the lemon with a knife removing the pith and the outside membranes. Wash the lettuce and the carrots. Put the ingredients through the juicer, alternating the beetroot and carrot to "rinse" the beetroot through with the firmer carrot. Season with salt and pepper and serve.

/ You can also use raw beetroot. /

x 4 to 6

/ Beetroot and Lettuce Risotto with Pecorino /

Preparation: 10 minutes
Cooking time: around 25 minutes

Ingredients

- 50 cl/18 fl oz/2 cups Red Salad Smoothie
- 300 g/10½ oz/1⅓ cup arborio rice or other risotto rice
- 125 g/4⅓ oz pecorino cheese
- 1 sweet onion
- 1 cooked beetroot
- ½ head lettuce
- 1 clove garlic
- 1 sprig fresh thyme
- a few sprigs parsley
- 25 cl/9 fl oz/1 cup vegetable or chicken stock, or diluted soup
- 1 dash olive oil
- salt and pepper

Peel the onion and garlic and chop finely. Cook them in the olive oil until soft but not brown. Add the rice and a sprig of thyme. Mix and add the stock. Allow the rice to absorb the liquid, and then add the Red Salad Smoothie little by little, allowing the rice to absorb it each time. Cut the beetroot into a small dice. Wash the lettuce and cut into strips. Chop the parsley. Grate the cheese. Just before the rice is finished cooking, add the grated cheese so it can melt. The risotto should be creamy. If needed, add juice, stock or water. Season with salt and pepper. Before serving, add the tomato dice and the chopped basil. Sprinkle with a dash of olive oil.

/ Sprinkle the risotto with chopped walnuts, hazelnuts or almonds. /

approx.
60 cl
1 ¼ pints
2 ½ cups

/ Go Green /

Ingredients

- 2 avocados
- 1 cucumber
- ½ green bell pepper
- ½ grapefruit
- salt and pepper

Peel the avocados and remove the pits. Peel the grapefruit with a knife, removing all the pith and outside membranes. Wash the cucumber and bell pepper. Remove the green pepper seeds. Put all the ingredients through the juicer. Season with salt and pepper and serve.

/ A cold soup that needs no cooking. /

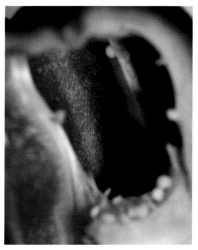

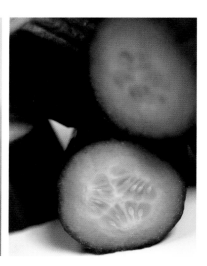

x 4

Preparation: 10 minutes
Cooking time: around 5 minutes

Ingredients

- 60 cl/1¼ pints/2½ cups Go Green juice
- 4 free range chicken breasts
- 2 tablespoons pistachios
- 1 small bunch fresh coriander leaves (cilantro)
- 1 small teaspoon curry powder
- salt and pepper

Cut the chicken breasts into strips or a dice. Adjust the cooking time depending on the size of the pieces. Pour the Go Green juice in a saucepan. Add the chopped fresh coriander leaves, heat over a low heat (50°C/122°F maximum). Add the chicken and the curry powder and continue cooking a few minutes. Add the pistachios before serving.

/ The avocado in the cooking liquid contains all the fat you need for the cooking. /
/ Serve with basmati rice, bulgur or spelt. /

approx.
60 cl
1 ¼ pints
2 ½ cups

/ Ice Garden Smoothie /

Ingredients

- ½ fennel bulb
- ½ green bell pepper
- 1 sweet apple (Golden)
- 1 small handful green beans
- 1 branch celery
- ½ lemon
- salt and pepper

Wash the vegetables and the apple, seed the green pepper, and remove the lemon peel with a knife cutting away the rind and the membrane. Juice all the ingredients. Season with salt and pepper and serve.

/ Serve this juice very cold, or even iced, directly out of the freezer. /

 x 4

/ Cod Steak Poached
in Ice Garden Smoothie /

Preparation: 15 minutes
Cooking time: around 20 minutes

Ingredients

- 60 cl/1¼ pints/2½ cups
  Iced Garden Smoothie
- 500 to 600 g/1 lb 2 oz to 1 lb 5 oz cod,
  whiting or other white fish
- 200 g/7 oz green beans
- 100 g/3½ oz/⅔ cup almonds
- a few sprigs fresh parsley
- 20 g/⅔ oz/1 heaped tablespoon
  salt butter
- salt and pepper

Remove the tips of the green beans and cut them in three. Pour the Iced Garden smoothie into a saucepan, add a little salt and the green beans. Cook for about 15 minutes over a low heat (50°C/120°F maximum). Chop the almonds roughly. Cut the fish into medium-sized cubes and poach in the juice. Add the chopped almonds and cook for 3 to 4 minutes. Serve with a little chopped parsley and a few shavings of salt butter.

/ Serve with steamed potatoes. /

approx.
50 cl
18 fl oz
2 cups

/ Booster Juice /

Ingredients

- 1 tart apple (Granny Smith)
- 1 sweet apple (Golden)
- ½ cucumber
- 1 lime
- 1 branch celery
- a few sprigs parsley (with stem)
- 1 tablespoon ground almond
  or ½ banana

Wash the fruit and vegetables, except the lemon, which should be peeled, removing the pith and the outer membranes. Juice all these ingredients. If you want to thicker juice, add a tablespoon of ground almonds or half a mashed banana. Serve.

/ Parsley is full of vitamin C. Don't hesitate to use it in morning juices. /

x 4 to 6

/ Boosted Salmon, Pea and Carrot Stew /

Preparation: 20 minutes
Cooking time: 20 minutes

Ingredients

- 50 cl/18 fl oz/2 cups Booster Juice
- 600 g/1 lb 5½ oz fresh salmon
- 500 g/1 lb 2 oz fresh peas
- 4 large carrots
- 10 pieces dried tomatoes
- 1 small bunch fresh coriander leaves (cilantro)
- 1 dash olive oil
- salt and pepper

Cut the salmon into medium-sized cubes. Shell the peas. Peel the carrots and slice thinly. Pour the Booster Juice into a saucepan. Add the carrots, the peas and the dried tomatoes. Season lightly. Cook for about 15 minutes over a low heat (50°C/120°F maximum) for about 15 minutes. Add the salmon and continue cooking for 5 minutes. Adjust the seasoning. Add a dash of olive oil, and then the chopped coriander leaves.

33

approx.
70 cl
1⅓ pints
3 cups

/ Radish & Co. /

Ingredients

- 2 large bunches radishes
- 4 carrots
- 1 tart apple (Granny Smith)
- 1 sweet apple (Golden)
- 1 small orange
- ½ grapefruit
- a few drops argan oil
- pepper

Peel the orange and grapefruit with a knife, removing the pith and all the outside membranes. Wash the other fruit and vegetables. Process all these ingredients through the juicer. Season each glass of juice with a few drops of argan oil and a little pepper.

/ Argan oil is not only renowned for its cosmetic virtues, but it is also wonderful in cooking. It is particularly rich in essential fatty acids, is very nutritional and highly flavoured. Use it with moderation. /

/ By adding apples to vegetable juice, you balance out the flavours so both the young and old will like vegetables. /

approx.
50 cl
18 fl oz
2 cups

/ Intense! /

Ingredients

- 1 large handful green beans
- 1 handful fresh mung bean sprouts
  (see page 12)
- 3 kiwis
- 1 small bunch parsley
- salt and pepper

Wash the vegetables and fruit, run them through the juicer, and then season lightly with salt and pepper. Serve and enjoy some intense greenery!

approx.
80 cl
1 ½ pints
3 ½ cups

/ Tomato Shock /

Ingredients

- 4 or 5 tomatoes (Pendelotte)
- 1 bulb fennel
- ½ pear
- ½ lemon
- A few sprigs fresh basil

Wash the tomatoes, fennel, pear and basil. Peel the lemon with a knife, removing the pith and outside membranes. Put all the ingredients through the centrifuge juicer and serve.

x 4 to 6

/ Tomato Shock and Fennel Tabouleh /

Preparation: 15 minutes
Set aside: 45 to 60 minutes

Ingredients

- 80 cl/1½ pints/3½ cups Tomato Shock juice
- 500 g/1 lb 2 oz/2⅓ cups of fine bulgur wheat
- 5 or 6 tomatoes
- 1 or 2 bulbs fennel
- a few tender celery ribs
- a few sprigs fresh basil
- 1 large handful black olives
- juice of 1 lemon
- 1 dash olive oil
- salt and pepper

Place the bulgur wheat in a bowl, pour in the Tomato Shock juice and set aside for 45 to 60 minutes. Wash the tomatoes and fennel. Cut into very fine pieces. Season the fennel with salt and pepper and sprinkle with lemon juice. Decorate the bulgur with tomato slices, fennel, celery and basil leaves. Add a few olives. Sprinkle with lemon juice and olive oil.

approx.
60 cl
1 ¼ pints
2 ½ cups

/ Martian Smoothie /

Ingredients

- 500 g/1 lb 2 oz honeydew melon
- 2 avocados
- ½ cucumber
- 1 lime

Peel and seed the honeydew melon. Peel the lemon with a knife, removing the pith and the outside membranes. Remove the avocado pits, without peeling them if the avocadoes have a thin green skin. Cut all the ingredients into large pieces and run them through the juicer, alternating the avocado with the other ingredients and ending with the melon in order to recuperate all the avocado juice. Serve and enjoy these out-of-this-world flavours.

/ Martian sherbet with maple syrup /

x 4 to 6

Preparation: 15 minutes in an ice cream machine or about 5 hours in the freezer

Ingredients

- 60 cl/1¼ pints/2½ cups Martian Smoothie
- a few tablespoons maple syrup

Pour the Martian Smoothie into the ice cream machine and freeze for about 15 minutes according to the manufacturer's instructions. Or, place it in a flat, stainless steal dish, which conducts the cold well, and freeze for 2 or 3 hours. Once it is hard, break up the preparation into pieces and process in a food processor until smooth. Return to the stainless steal dish and freeze for at least another 2 hours. Serve the sherbet in glasses or bowls. Douse with maple syrup.

approx.
60 cl
1 ¼ pints
2 ½ cups

/ Three in One /

Ingredients

- 2 or 3 handfuls fresh mung bean sprouts (see page 12)
- 4 or 5 carrots
- 3 oranges

x 4 to 6

Preparation: 20 minutes
Set aside: 45 to 60 minutes

Ingredients

- 60 cl/1¼ pints/2½ cups Three in One juice
- 400 g/14 oz/1⅔ cups fine bulgur wheat
- 1 bunch fresh watercress
- 4 large carrots
- 2 green bell peppers
- 100 g/3½ oz/⅔ cup raisins
- 1 lime
- 1 dash olive oil
- salt and pepper

/ Serve the tabouleh with a fresh bean sprout salad. /

Peel the oranges with a knife, removing the pith and the outside membrane. Wash the carrots and the bean sprouts. Put everything in the juicer.

/ Three in One Vegy Tabouleh /

Place the bulgur wheat in a bowl, pour in the Three in One juice and set aside for 45 to 60 minutes. Put the raisins in a saucepan, cover with water, bring to a boil, remove from heat and set aside until the raisins are plump. Put the dried tomatoes in a saucepan, cover with water, bring to a boil, cook for 4 to 5 minutes, and then drain. Put them in the olive oil with some lemon juice to marinate. Wash the watercress, green peppers and carrots. Grate the carrots. Remove the seeds from the green peppers and cut into thin slices. Chop the dried tomatoes. Mix all these ingredients with the plumped bulgur. Season with salt and pepper. Put the tabouleh in a serving bowl, surrounded by watercress. Add the raisins and the lime, cut into sections. Sprinkle with olive oil.

approx.
50 cl
18 fl oz
2 cups

/ Morning Wake-up /

Ingredients

- 8 or 9 young carrots
- 1 apple
- ½ lemon

/ This is a simple, effective waker-upper for the morning. /

Wash the carrots and the apple. Peel the lemon removing the pith and the outside membranes. Process everything through the juicer. Serve.

/ Eat Your Heart Out /

Ingredients

- 3 or 4 "Coeur de boeuf" (beefheart) ribbed tomatoes
- ½ cucumber
- 1 sweet apple (Golden)

Wash all the ingredients and juice them. Serve.

/ Coeur de boeuf or beefheart tomatoes are large tomatoes named for their shape. They are delicious, refined and have practically no seeds. Like most tomatoes, they are good raw or cooked, alone or with other vegetables. /

approx.
50 cl
18 fl oz
2 cups

/ Sweet and Savoury /

Ingredients

- 1 cantaloupe
- 2 branches celery
- ½ red bell pepper
- ½ lemon
- salt and pepper

Peel and seed the cantaloupe. Use a knife to peel the lemon, removing the skin, pith and outer membrane. Wash the celery and pepper. Seed the latter. Put all the ingredients through the juicer. Season with salt and pepper and serve.

/ Choose cantaloupes that are heavy, full of sun and very sweet. You can tell the melon is ripe if the skin is slightly bursting around the stem, and the stem is ready to come off. Open your eyes. /

x 4 to 5

Preparation: 5 minutes
Freeze: 15 minutes in an ice cream
machine or about 5 hours in the freezer

Ingredients

- 50 cl/18 fl oz/2 cups Sweet and
  Savoury juice
- a few pieces dark chocolate
  (70% cocoa solids)
- 1 dash olive oil

Pour the Sweet and Savoury juice into the ice cream machine
and freeze for about 15 minutes according to the manufacturer's
instructions. Or, place it in a flat, stainless steal dish, which conducts
the cold well, and freeze for 2 or 3 hours. Once it is hard, break up
the preparation into pieces and process in a food processor until
smooth. Return to the stainless steal dish and freeze for at least
another 2 hours. Serve the sherbet in bowls or emptied out half-
melons, sprinkle with olive oil and grated chocolate.

approx.
60 cl
1 ¼ pints
2 ½ cups

/ Summer Colour Cooler /

Ingredients

- 2 tomatoes
- 1 red bell pepper
- 1 apple
- 1 blood orange or regular orange
- ½ lemon

Peel the oranges and lemon using a knife, removing the skin, pith and outer membranes. Wash the tomatoes, apple and bell pepper. Seed the latter. Juice all the ingredients. Serve.

x 6 to 8

/ Summer Colour Carrot and Potato Soup /

Preparation: 10 minutes
Cooking time: 25 minutes

Ingredients

- 60 cl/1¼ pints/2½ cups
  Summer Colour Cooler
- 500 g/1 lb 2 oz carrots
- 1 kg/2 lb 4 oz mashing potatoes
- 1 dash olive oil
- salt and pepper

Peel the vegetables and cook them in a little water. Once they are cooked, drain and put them back in the pot and mash with a hand-held masher. Right before serving, pour freshly prepared Summer Colour Cooler over the hot vegetable mash. Season with salt and pepper and sprinkle with olive oil.

/ By pouring the cold juice over the hot mash, it is just barely warmed, which means it keeps all its vitamins. /

approx.
50 cl
18 fl oz
2 cups

/ China Peppers /

Ingredients

- 1 red bell pepper
- 1 nashi pear (Asian pear)
- ½ bulb fennel
- ½ lemon

Peel the lemon with a knife, removing the skin, pith and outer membranes. Wash the nashi pear, the fennel and the pepper. Seed the latter. Put everything in the juicer. Serve.

/ The nashi pear originated in Far Eastern temperate regions. It is also called Japanese pear, Korean pear, apple pear and sand pear. This fruit is both crunchy and juicy. /

x 4 or 5

Preparation: 20 minutes
Set aside: at least 2 hours

Ingredients

- 50 cl/18 fl oz/2 cups China Peppers juice
- 1 grapefruit per person

/ China Pepper Granita in Grapefruit /

Pour the China Peppers juice in a flat, stainless steel recipient and put it in the freezer for 2 to 3 hours. Once the preparation freezes, use a fork to scrape of flakes. Serve this granita or keep it in the freezer. Cut a slice off the bottom of the grapefruits so they are stable, and cut a slice off the top to form a cover. Empty the grapefruit using a little knife and cut the fruit into thin slices. Place these in the emptied grapefruit skin, with a large scoop of granita and top with the cover.

approx.
80 cl
1 ½ pints
3 ½ cups

/ Beach Bali /

Ingredients

- 1 pineapple
- 1 apple
- 1 bouquet fresh mint
- 3 tablespoons ground almond
- 2 teaspoons pistachios
- 2 slices candied ginger
- a few drops of lime juice

Peel the pineapple. Wash the apple and the mint. Put the fruit through the juicer with half the mint. Add the almond powder. Flavour with a little lime juice. Chop the pistachios and the candied ginger. Chop the remaining mint and add to the juice. Serve in glasses and decorate with the chopped pistachios and ginger.

/ In Bali, you find pineapple served with generous quantities of mint. If the pineapple is not ripe enough, add a tablespoon of honey to the juice. You can also add candied or dried pineapple. /

x 4 to 6

/ Beach Bali Sherbet with pistachios and caramelized almonds /

Preparation: 5 minutes
Freeze: 15 minutes in an ice cream machine or about 5 hours in the freezer

Ingredients

- 80 cl/1½ pints/3½ cups Beach Bali juice
- 2 handfuls pistachios
- 1 handful unpeeled almonds
- 1 large tablespoon unrefined cane sugar
- 1 lump butter

Pour the Beach Bali juice into the ice cream machine and freeze for about 15 minutes according to the manufacturer's instructions. Or, place it in a flat, stainless steal dish, which conducts the cold well, and freeze for 2 or 3 hours. Once it is hard, break up the preparation into pieces and process in a food processor until smooth. Return to the stainless steal dish and freeze for at least another 2 hours. Melt the butter in a skillet with the sugar. Add the almonds and caramelize for 1 to 2 minutes. Cool and chop into large pieces. Serve the sherbet decorated with pistachios and almonds.

approx.
60 cl
1 ¼ pints
2 ½ cups

/ Cherry Elixir /

Ingredients

- 500 g/1 lb 2 oz cherries
- 1 nashi pear (Asian pear)
- 1 sweet apple (Golden)
- 1 handful fresh mung bean sprouts (see page 12)
- ½ lime
- 1 package vanilla sugar

Wash the fruit and the bean sprouts. Peel the lime with a knife removing the skin, pith and outer membranes. Process all these ingredients through the juicer. Place the cherries in the juicer whole before turning it on. Add the vanilla sugar to the juice and serve.

/ If you do not have nashi pears, use one or two apples or pears. /

/ Thick Cherry and Soy Milkshake /

x 4 to 6

Preparation: 5 minutes
Freeze: around 30 minutes

Ingredients

- 60 cl/1¼ pints/2½ cups Cherry Elixir juice
- 4 soymilk yogurts

Put the yogurts in the freezer until they are hard. Place them in a food processor with the Cherry Elixir juice. Blend and serve cold.

approx.
90 cl/just
under 2 pts
4 cups

/ Winter-Summer
China Style Smoothie /

Ingredients

- 4 peaches
- 4 or 5 carrots
- 2 oranges
- 1 stick fresh lemongrass
  (Asian specialty stores)
- 1 small piece fresh ginger

Wash the peaches and carrots. Cut the peaches in two and remove the pits. Peel the oranges removing the peel, pith and membranes. Put all the ingredients through the juicer and serve.

/ Lemongrass is very popular among Thai and Vietnamese cooks, who use it to flavour many dishes. Fresh lemon grass will keep 4 to 5 days in the bottom vegetable compartment in the refrigerator. If you can't find fresh lemongrass, frozen lemongrass is a good substitute, unlike dried lemon grass, which has little flavour. /

61

/ China Style Peach and Mint Tabouleh /

Preparation: 20 minutes
Set aside: 45 to 60 minutes

Ingredients

- 90 cl/just under 2 pints/4 cups Winter-Summer China Style Smoothie
- 500 g/1 lb 2 oz/2⅓ cups fine bulgur wheat
- 4 peaches
- 4 oranges
- 2 handfuls pistachios
- 1 large handful raisins
- a few slices dried banana
- 1 piece fresh or candied ginger (optional)
- honey
- a few fresh mint leaves
- juice of 1 orange or ½ lemon
- 1 dash olive oil

Place the bulgur wheat in a bowl, pour in the Winter-Summer China Style Smoothie and set aside for 45 to 60 minutes. Put the raisins in a saucepan with 1 or 2 tablespoons honey and a little water. Bring to a boil, remove from heat and set aside until the raisins are plump. Peel the oranges with a knife, removing the skin, pith and membranes. Cut into slices. Cut the peaches into sections. Present the bulgur with the orange slices and peach sections. Add the pistachios, the dried banana slices and the honey-plumped raisins, and then decorate with mint leaves. Sprinkle with orange or lemon juice and a dash of olive oil. Add a dribble of honey and serve with fresh or candied ginger to taste.

approx.
90 cl/just
under 2 pts
4 cups

/ Indian Summer Smoothie /

Ingredients

- 1 large bunch green grapes
- 3 pears
- 2 kiwis + 1 for decoration
- ½ lemon
- a few fresh mint leaves

Wash the fruit. Be sure to scrub the kiwis well. Remove the grapes from the stems and put them through the juicer with the pears and two kiwis. Decorate the glasses of juice with thin slices of peeled kiwi and a mint leaf. Sprinkle with a few drops of lemon to keep the juice from turning brown.

x 4 to 6

Preparation: 10 minutes
Freeze: at least 2 hours

/ Indian Summer Granita with Honey Raisins /

Ingredients

- 90 cl/just under 2 pints/4 cups Indian Summer Smoothie
- 2 large handful raisins
- 2 to 3 tablespoons honey

Pour the Indian Summer Smoothie in a flat, stainless steel recipient and put it in the freezer for 2 to 3 hours. Once the preparation freezes, use a fork to scrape off flakes. Serve this granita or keep it in the freezer. Put the raisins in a saucepan with 2 or 3 tablespoons honey and cover with water. Bring to a boil, remove from heat and set aside until the raisins are plump. Serve the granita with a few raisins and a small teaspoon of honey.

/ You can choose green or black raisons, depending on your mood. Kiwi provides a good dose of vitamin C and adds a touch of acidity to the pear's sweetness. /

approx.
60 cl
1 ¼ pints
2 ½ cups

/ Prickly... /

Ingredients

- 4 prickly pear cactus fruits
- 4 plums
- 2 small apples
- 1 small bunch green grapes
- ½ lime

Peel the prickly pear cactus fruit and the lemon. Wash the grapes, apples and plums. Pit the latter. Put all these ingredients through the juicer. Serve.

/ Prickly pear cactus fruits are oval shaped and can be either a more or less dark purple or yellow green with a little red. They contain a juicy, sweet pulp of the same colour and filled with little seeds. Prickly pear cactus fruit is rich in vitamin C. There are several varieties that have thorns, which should be removed, with or without the skin, before you eat the fruit, which is usually served cold. /

approx.
70 cl
1⅓ pints
3 cups

/ Candy Pink /

Ingredients

- **300 g/10½ oz raspberries**
- **3 pears (William)**
- **½ grapefruit**

Wash the raspberries, quickly to keep them from filling with water. Wash the pears. Peel the grapefruit with a knife, removing the skin, pith and membranes. Put all the ingredients through the juicer and serve.

 x 4 to 6

/ Raspberry Cubes /

Preparation: 10 minutes
Set aside: around 30 minutes

Ingredients

- **70 cl/1⅓ pints/3 cups Candy Pink juice**
- **250 g/9 oz raspberries**
- **1 tablespoon maple syrup**
- **1 teaspoon agar agar powder (see page 8)**
- **1 package vanilla sugar**

Wash the raspberries, quickly to keep them from filling with water. Heat half of the Candy Pink juice with the maple syrup and the vanilla sugar, until simmering, a little before it boils (about 80°C/175°F). Add the agar agar powder and whisk. Remove from heat, add the rest of the juice and mix well. Pour into a dish large enough to make cubes the desired thickness. Add the raspberries. Allow to cool and cut into cubes or strips.

/ Champagne version: follow the same recipe, using half juice and half champagne, added cold. /

approx.
60 cl
1 ¼ pints
2 ½ cups

/ Candy Red /

Ingredients

- 300 g/10½ oz strawberries
- 3 small carrots
- ¼ pineapple

Wash the strawberries. Peel the pineapple. Wash the carrots.
Put all the ingredients through the juicer and serve.

 x 4 to 6

/ Strawberry cubes /

Preparation: 10 minutes
Set aside: around 30 minutes

Ingredients

- 60 cl/1¼ pints/2½ cups Candy Red juice
- 200 g/7 oz strawberries
- 1 tablespoon maple syrup
- 1 teaspoon agar agar powder (see page 8)
- 1 package vanilla sugar
- a few fresh mint leaves

Wash the strawberries quickly, remove the stems, and cut them in two or three pieces depending on their size. Heat half of the juice with the maple syrup and the vanilla sugar, until simmering, a little before it boils (about 80°C/175°F). Add the agar agar powder and whisk. Remove from heat, add the rest of the juice and mix well. Pour into a dish large enough to make cubes the desired thickness. Add the strawberries and the mint leaves. Leave them to cool and cut into cubes or strips (see photo below).

/ Champagne version: follow the same recipe, using half juice and half champagne, added cold. /

approx.
70 cl
1⅓ pints
3 cups

/ Bali Bali Smoothie /

Ingredients

- 3 avocados
- 2 sweet apples (Golden)
- 2 clementines
- 2 oranges
- 2 tablespoons bitter cocoa powder

Peel the clementines and oranges with a knife, removing the skin, pith and outside membranes. Remove the avocado pits, without peeling them if the avocadoes have a thin green skin. Wash the apples. Cut all the ingredients into large pieces and run them through the juicer, alternating the avocado with the other ingredients and ending with the apple in order to recuperate all the avocado juice. Add the cocoa powder. Mix and serve.

/ The avocado is a deliciously smooth fruit. Here is a daring marriage with bitter chocolate. /

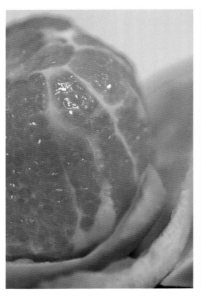

approx.
80 cl
1⅓ pints
3 ½ cups

/ Pink /

Ingredients

- 500 g/1 lb 2 oz strawberries
- 500 g/1 lb 2 oz honeydew melon
- ½ lime
- a few sprigs fresh basil

Peel and seed the honeydew melon. Peel the lemon with a knife, removing the pith and the outside membranes. Put everything through the juicer. Serve and sprinkle the glasses with chopped basil.

approx.
80 cl
1 ½ pints
3 ½ cups

/ Yo papaya! /

Ingredients

- 1 papaya
- 500 g/1 lb 2 oz honeydew melon
- 1 sweet apple (Golden)
- 1 small piece fresh ginger

Peel the melon and the papaya, removing the largest seeds. Wash the apple. Put all these ingredients through the juicer. Serve.

x 4 or 5

/ Yo, Papaya Popsicles /

Preparation: 15 minutes in an ice cream machine or about 5 hours in the freezer

Ingredients

- 80 cl/1½ pints/3½ cups Yo, Papaya juice

Freeze the juice for about 15 minutes in an ice cream machine according to manufacturer's instructions, and then put into stick-shaped moulds. Or, place the juice in a flat, stainless steal dish, which conducts the cold well, and freeze for 2 or 3 hours. Once it is hard, break up the preparation into pieces and process in a food processor until smooth. Put in the moulds and freeze for at least another 2 hours.

approx.
60 cl
1 ¼ pints
2 ½ cups

/ In the Vines /

Ingredients

- ½ cantaloupe
- 1 large bunch black grapes
- 1 banana
- ½ lemon
- 5 cl/1¾ fl oz/¼ cup coconut milk

Peel the melon, banana and lemon. Remove the melon seeds. Wash the grapes and remove the stems. Put everything through the juicer, starting with the banana, so that the juice from the other fruit "rinses" it through. Add the coconut milk. Mix and serve.

/ Eat grapes! Their virtues have been celebrated since antiquity. Grape cures have been reputed for decades for regenerating the body… so don't hesitate. /

approx.
60 cl
1 ¼ pints
2 ½ cups

/ Happy Banana Smoothie /

Ingredients

- 4 bananas
- 2 oranges
- 4 clementines
- ½ lime
- 1 dried banana
- 2 pieces candied ginger
- ½ vanilla pod

Peel the citrus fruit with a knife, removing the skin, pith and membranes. Peel the banana. Split the vanilla pod lengthwise and scrape out the seeds. Put the fruit through the juicer and then add the vanilla seeds. Whisk. Cut the dried banana and candied ginger into strips and use them to decorate the glasses of juice.

x 4 or 5

/ Happy Banana Ice Cream with Condensed Milk /

Preparation: 5 minutes
Freeze: 15 minutes in an ice cream machine or about 5 hours in the freezer

Ingredients

- 60 cl/1¼ pints/2½ cups Happy Banana Smoothie
- 1 tube unsweetened condensed milk
- 1 handful dried banana slices
- 1 large handful Amaretto biscuits

Mix together the Happy Banana Smoothie and the condensed milk. Freeze the mixture for 15 minutes in an ice cream machine following the manufacturer's instructions. Two or three minutes before the end, add the dried banana pieces and the Amaretto biscuits, broken into pieces. Or, place it in a flat, stainless steal dish, which conducts the cold well, and freeze for 2 or 3 hours. Once it is hard, break up the preparation into pieces and process in a food processor until smooth. Return to the stainless steal dish and freeze for at least another 2 hours. When the ice cream is nearly finished freezing, about an hour after having blended it, add the dried banana and Amaretto biscuit pieces.

approx.
60 cl
1 ¼ pints
2 ½ cups

/ Mellow Yellow /

Ingredients

- 400 g/14 oz honeydew melon
- 1 grapefruit
- ½ pear (William)
- ½ tart apple (Granny Smith)
- 1 small piece fresh ginger
- ½ stick fresh lemongrass
  (Asian specialty stores)
- 1 dash curcuma

Peel and seed the melon. Peel the grapefruit with a knife, removing the skin, pith and membranes. Wash the pear and apple. Put all the fruit through the juicer, along with the ginger and lemon grass. Add the curcuma. Serve.

 x 4

/ Mellow Yellow Banana Milkshake /

Preparation: 5 minutes
Freeze: around 30 minutes

Ingredients

- 60 cl/1¼ pints/2½ cups
  Mellow Yellow juice
- 4 soymilk yogurts

Put the yogurts in the freezer until they are hard. Place them in a food processor with the Mellow Yellow juice. Blend and serve cold.

approx.
60 cl
1 ¼ pints
2 ½ cups

/ Melon & Mango /

Ingredients

- ½ cantaloupe
- 200 to 300 g/7 to 10½ oz honeydew melon
- ½ mango
- ½ grapefruit
- ½ lemon

Peel and seed the melons. Peel the mango. Peel the grapefruit and the lemon using a knife and removing the skin, pith and membrane. Put all these ingredients through the juicer. Serve.

/ Melon & Mango Sherbet /

x 4 or 5

Preparation: 15 minutes
Freeze: 15 minutes in an ice cream machine or about 5 hours in the freezer

Ingredients

- 60 cl/1¼ pints/2½ Melon & Mango juice
- 1 mango
- 1 cantaloupe
- juice of ½ lime

Pour the Melon & Mango juice into the ice cream machine and freeze for about 15 minutes according to the manufacturer's instructions. Or, place it in a flat, stainless steal dish, which conducts the cold well, and freeze for 2 or 3 hours. Once it is hard, break up the preparation into pieces and process in a food processor until smooth. Return to the stainless steal dish and freeze for at least another 2 hours. Peel and seed the melon. Blend it into a thick juice and flavour with lime juice. Peel the mango and cut into strips. Serve the sherbet with the mango strips and coated with the melon sauce.

approx.
50 cl
18 fl oz
2 cups

/ Piña Colada /

Ingredients

- ½ large pineapple
- 25 cl/9 fl oz/1 cup coconut milk
- 10 cl/3½ fl oz/²⁄₅ cup white rum
- 5 cl/1¾ fl oz/¼ cup cane syrup
- ½ vanilla pod

Peel the pineapple and run it through the juicer. Split the vanilla pod lengthwise and scrape out the seeds. Add the coconut milk, rum, cane syrup and vanilla seeds to the pineapple juice. Whisk. Serve with ice cubes or crushed ice if you prefer really cold cocktails.

x 4 to 6

/ Piña Colada Sherbet with Pineapple and Coconut /

Preparation: 5 minutes
Freeze: 15 minutes in an ice cream machine or about 5 hours in the freezer

Ingredients

- 50 cl/18 fl oz/2 cups piña colada
- ¼ fresh pineapple
- a few slices of sugared coconut (Asian specialty stores)
- 20 cl/7 fl oz/⁴⁄₅ cup coconut milk

Pour the Piña Colada into the ice cream machine and freeze for about 15 minutes according to the manufacturer's instructions. Or, place it in a flat, stainless steal dish, which conducts the cold well, and freeze for 2 or 3 hours. Once it is hard, break up the preparation into pieces and process in a food processor until smooth. Return to the stainless steal dish and freeze for at least another 2 hours. Peel the pineapple and cut it into thin slices. Pour a little coconut milk into the bottom of the serving dish. Add scoops of sherbet and serve with fresh pineapple slices and coconut slices.

/ You can use either ready-made coconut milk or make it yourself by putting fresh coconut through the centrifuge juicer. /

approx.
50 cl
18 fl oz
2 cups

/ Sunny Cognac /

Ingredients

- 1 large mango
- 4 or 5 carrots
- ½ lime
- 10 cl/3½ oz/⅘ cup vanilla-flavoured cognac

Wash the carrots. Cut the mango in four and remove the pit. Peel the mango quarters and the lemon. Put all these ingredients through the juicer. Flavour with vanilla cognac. Serve.

/ I use Meukow VS Vanilla cognac to make this cocktail. Serve with ice cubes or crushed ice if you prefer really cold cocktails. You can also create a variation with Schweppes. /

approx.
60 cl
1 ¼ pint
2 ½ cups

/ Cocktail for Geneviève /

Ingredients

- 2 kiwis
- ¼ pineapple
- 1 tart apple (Granny Smith)
- 1 sweet apple (Golden)
- 1 piece lemongrass (Asian stores)
- 10 cl/3½ oz/⅖ cup cognac

Peel the pineapple. Wash the apples and kiwis, scrubbing the latter well. Put the fruit and the lemongrass through the juicer and mix with the cognac. Serve.

/ This cocktail is flavoured with Frapin cognac, in homage to Geneviève Cointreau who, for a long time, participated in developing these nectars. She was a marvellous woman whom I admire greatly... and she was a descendent of François Rabelais no less! /

x 4 to 6

/ Geneviève's Sherbet with Pineapple Syrup /

Preparation: 15 minutes
Freeze: 15 minutes in an ice cream machine or about 5 hours in the freezer

Ingredients

- 60 cl/1¼ pints/2½ cups Cocktail for Geneviève
- ½ pineapple
- 150 g/5¼ oz /⅔ cups unrefined cane sugar (organically grown)
- a few fresh mint leaves

Pour the Cocktail for Geneviève into the ice cream machine and freeze for about 15 minutes according to the manufacturer's instructions. Or, place it in a flat, stainless steal dish, which conducts the cold well, and freeze for 2 or 3 hours. Once it is hard, break up the preparation into pieces and process in a food processor until smooth. Return to the stainless steal dish and freeze for at least another 2 hours. Present the sherbet in an emptied pineapple. Put the half pineapple through the juicer and heat the juice with the sugar. Reduce by half. Cool and pour over the sherbet to serve. Decorate with mint leaves.

/ An Island in Charentes /

Ingredients

- 1 papaya
- 1 tart apple (Granny Smith)
- 2 oranges
- ½ lime
- 10 cl/3½ oz/⅖ cup cognac

Peel the apple, and then the oranges and lemon using a knife, removing the skin, pith and outer membranes. Peel the papaya and remove the large seeds. Put all these ingredients through the juicer. Flavour with cognac. Serve.

/ Bache-Gabrielsen cognac brings out the flavours of the papaya, which I enjoyed in quantity in the Caribbean, which I remember with this tropical-Scandinavian blend. Serve with ice cubes or crushed ice if you prefer really cold cocktails. /

approx.
50 cl
18 fl oz
2 cups

/ Poolside Power Pastis /

Ingredients

- 1 bulb fennel
- 1 tart apple (Granny Smith)
- 10 cl/3½ fl oz/⅖ cup pastis

Wash the fennel and the apple. Put them through the juicer. Flavour with pastis. Decorate with sprigs of fennel tops and serve with crushed ice if you want to.

x 4 to 6

Preparation: 10 minutes
Freeze: 1 hour

Ingredients

Positive:
- 50 cl/18 fl oz/2 cups Poolside Power Pastis
- 4 or 5 tomatoes
- 1 celery rib
- celery salt

Negative:
- 50 cl/18 fl oz/2 cups Poolside Power Pastis
- 4 or 5 tomatoes
- 1 celery rib
- celery salt

/ Opposites: Tomato Pastis Cocktails /

Put the tomatoes and the celery through the juicer and season with celery salt. Pour into an ice tray and freeze. Serve the Poolside Power Pastis cooled with tomato ice cubes. Do the opposite for the ìnegativeî cocktail: make ice cubes with the Poolside Power Pastis. Make juice with the other ingredients and serve with the pastis ice cubes.

Acknowledgements

Thank you to all the artisans and producers who work the "gold of the earth", natural fruits and vegetables for a better life.

Thank you to Yves Delzenne and Laurent Naslot of the Rivera & Bar, who accepted to support this book, allowing me to give life to my memories of natural "potions" I have loved so much since childhood. Today, the tools that have been produced to make cooking easier are often an opportunity to eat a more healthy diet if you know how and why you use them! I give homage to Raymond Oliver, a grand master of French cuisine, who in the 1970s thanked the progress made in modern technology, saying it was not a bad thing at a time when many cooks were not yet ready to evolve…

I would like to thank my editor, Jean-Pierre Duval, who allowed me to complete this book that I wanted to write for so long and, above all, who took up the challenge of using fun to touch on a subject as serious as health. Thank you to Marie-Alexandre Perraud for knowing how to write down my recipes, which makes me love them even more. Thank you to our young and talented photographer, Valentin Duval, who is always surprising us with his fresh ideas and very high-tech techno perspectives. Good work!

Thank you to my friends, the talented artists Laurent Émeraud for creating my workshop, Roland Mellan (www.via.asso.fr) for his artwork, Marie for my wonderful t-shirts (www.be-myself.net). And also Christophe Deguillaume, my favourite painter, Roland Bellier (www.rolandbellier.20mn.com) for his bronze sculptures and Nahmias Ceramicas for the earthenware fish. Thanks again to Édouard Cointreau, who is always at my side. Thank you to the artisans who support me, and especially IVV and its glassware. Thank you to Michel Oliver, my master and reference in all things related to cookbooks. Thank you to my mother Yvette for her inspiration and recommendations.

This book is—once again, but never too many times—dedicated to my daughter Alta and to all the children, mothers and fathers who work every day in their kitchens to make others happy!

Yvan Cadiou, taste sculptor/www.yvancadiou.com

Editorial director / Marie-Alexandre Perraud
Graphic design / Maevi Colomina & Romain Pages Publishing
Photography / Valentin and Jean-Pierre Duval
Translation / Anne Trager
Printing and binding / Delo Tiskarna, Slovenia, Europe
First published in French in 2007, by Romain Pages Editions, France.

ISBN no. 978-1-906909-00-0

Romain Pages Publishing
Lincoln House
300 High Holborn
WC1V 7JH - London
United Kingdom
enquiries@romain-pages.co.uk
www.romain-pages.co.uk

Romain Pages Editions
BP 82030
30252 Sommières cedex
France
e.mail : contact@romain-pages.com
www.romain-pages.com